W9-AEM-174

My Muscles

by Rena Korb

illustrated by Rémy Simard

Content Consultant:
Anthony J. Weinhaus, PhD
Assistant Professor of Integrative Biology and Physiology
University of Minnesota

visit us at www.abdopublishing.com

Printed in the United States of America, North Mankato, Minnesota.
022010
092010

 THIS BOOK CONTAINS AT LEAST 10% RECYCLED MATERIALS.

Text by Rena Korb
Illustrations by Rémy Simard
Edited by Holly Saari
Interior layout and design by Emily Love
Cover design by Emily Love

Library of Congress Cataloging-in-Publication Data
Korb, Rena B.
  My muscles / by Rena Korb ; illustrated by Remy Simard ; Content Consultant, Anthony J. Weinhaus.
      p. cm. — (My body)
  Includes index.
  ISBN 978-1-60270-807-5
  1. Muscles—Juvenile literature. I. Simard, Rémy, ill. II. Weinhaus, Anthony J. III. Title.
  QP321.K67 2011
  612.7'4—dc22
                              2009048320

Table of Contents

My Muscles

Hi! I'm Sam. Check out my strong muscles! They keep my body going. They also let me jump and yell. Let's learn more about muscles!

My muscles move my arms and legs. They let me blink and talk. They also make my stomach and heart work. I have about 650 muscles.

Usually, about half of a person's weight comes from muscles. If you weigh 60 pounds (27 kg), you have almost 30 pounds (14 kg) of muscle!

My body has three types of muscles. Most of them are skeletal muscles. These connect to my skeleton, or bones. One end of the muscle joins to one bone. The other end joins to another bone.

Tendons are tough cords that connect skeletal muscles to bones.

I control my skeletal muscles. So, I decide when to use them. When I use a muscle, it contracts. This means it gets shorter.

Skeletal muscles are very powerful. But they get tired easily.

9

Skeletal muscles work in pairs. One muscle contracts. It pulls a bone in one direction. Then the other muscle contracts. It moves the bone back again.

Skeletal muscles heat up when they move. That is why people get warm when they move around a lot.

My biceps and triceps are a pair of muscles in my arm. I contract my biceps to bring my fork to my mouth. I contract my triceps to move my fork away from my mouth.

Some of the biggest muscles are in the back. They help keep the back straight when sitting and standing.

I contract my muscles to do lots of things. My thigh muscles work to run. My hand muscles go into action when I play the piano.

A muscle can cramp from being worked too hard. Cramps can be painful. But they only last a short time.

The muscles in my face do not connect bone to bone. They connect bone to skin. They move my skin so I can smile and frown.

Face muscles help people chew and show feelings.

Another type of muscle is called smooth muscle. It controls breathing, digesting, and other things my body does by itself. I don't need to tell myself to breathe so I can play soccer. I breathe without even thinking about it.

Smooth muscles use less energy than skeletal muscles.

Smooth muscle is in my blood vessels. It helps move my blood through my arteries and veins.

Many smooth muscles are as thin as a piece of string.

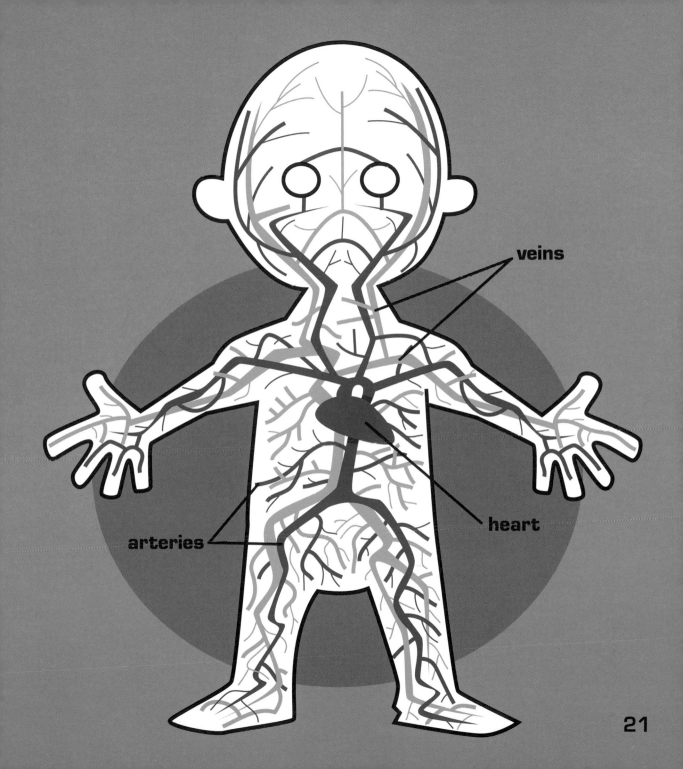

veins

heart

arteries

21

My stomach uses smooth muscles.
They contract and mash up any food
I eat. Smooth muscles are needed to
help me digest.

When a person's stomach
rumbles and gurgles,
the stomach muscles are
moving.

stomach

Another type of muscle I can't control is my cardiac muscle. That's only in my heart. Pump, pump! It's always hard at work.

People can change the speed of their heartbeats. Running up and down stairs will make the heart pump faster.

heart

My cardiac muscle contracts to pump blood out of my heart. The blood goes to the rest of my body. Then the muscles relax to let the blood back into my heart. That's one heartbeat.

Your heart contracts and relaxes more than 100,000 times a day. That's more than 2.5 billion times in a lifetime!

The heart contracts and blood goes to the body.

The heart relaxes and blood comes back to the heart.

27

Muscles help me move in fun ways. They also keep my body working. My muscles are hard at work when I play and rest!

Babies learn to control muscles as they grow. As they get older, they learn to sit up, crawl, and walk.

A Look Inside

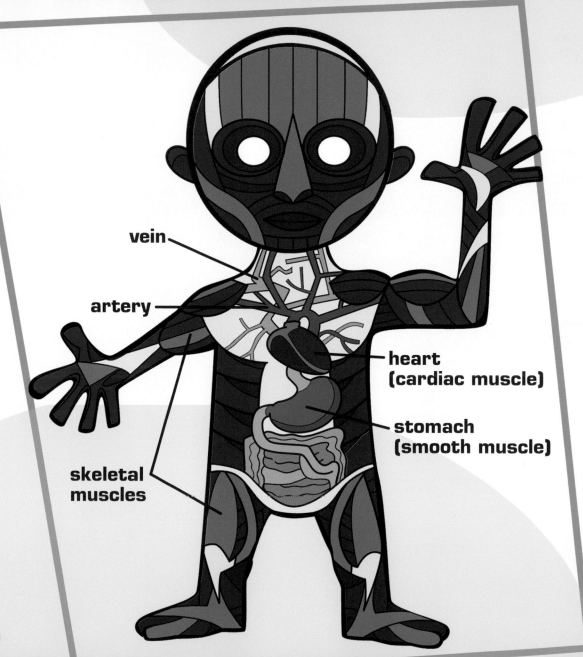

vein

artery

heart
(cardiac muscle)

stomach
(smooth muscle)

skeletal
muscles

Fun Facts

• Your eyeball has six muscles that connect to it. These muscles make the eye move up and down, from side to side, and diagonally. Your eyeball also has muscles inside it. These muscles help your eye focus and see better.

• Your bladder has smooth muscles. They help you hold your urine, or pee, until you can go to the bathroom. Then, smooth muscles push the urine out of your body.

Glossary

cardiac muscle – the muscle of the heart.

contract – to squeeze together to become smaller or shorter.

cramp – a painful contraction of a muscle.

relax – to make loose or less tight.

skeletal muscle – muscle that is attached to the skeleton.

skeleton – the bones inside the body.

smooth muscle – muscle that is found in the stomach, blood vessels, and other hollow body parts.

On the Web

To learn more about muscles, visit ABDO Group online at **www.abdopublishing.com**. Web sites about muscles are featured on our Book Links page. These links are routinely monitored and updated to provide the most current information available.

Index